D1068063

PERSON TO PERSON

Other Books by JOHN CIARDI

Homeward to America
Other Skies
Live Another Day
Mid-Century Poets
From Time to Time
Dante's Inferno
As If, Poems New and Selected
I Marry You
In the Stoneworks
39 Poems
Dante's Purgatorio
How Does a Poem Mean?
In Fact
Dialogue with an Audience
Poetry, a Closer Look
  (*with Reid and Perrine*)

Children's Verse

The Reason for the Pelican
Scappy the Pup
I Met a Man
The Man Who Sang the Sillies
The Wish Tree
You Read to Me, I'll Read to You
John J. Plenty and Fiddler Dan
You Know Who

PS3503
I27
P4

PERSON TO PERSON

JOHN CIARDI

RUTGERS UNIVERSITY PRESS

New Brunswick, New Jersey

95240

FEB 1965

Copyright © 1964 by Rutgers, The State University

Library of Congress Catalog Card Number: 64-18873

Manufactured in the United States of America
by Quinn & Boden Co., Inc., Rahway, New Jersey

ACKNOWLEDGMENTS

Some of these poems have previously been published in *The Atlantic, Saturday Review, Ladies Home Journal, The Nation, The Colorado Quarterly Review, Creative America* (Ridge Press), *Calliope* (Western Michigan University) and the *Tuftonian* (Tufts University).

8115
C48p.

To Irving and Ruth Klompus, persons, personally.

Contents

WHOLLY NUMBERS or THE MEDITATIONS OF ST. STITCH

PERSON TO PERSON

THE SIZE OF SONG

Some rule of birds kills off the song
in any that begin to grow
much larger than a fist or so.
What happens as they move along
to power and size? Something goes wrong.
Bird music is the tremolo
of the tremulous. Birds let us know
the songsters never are the strong.

One step more on the way of things,
we find a second rule applies
to birds that grow to such a size
they lose, or start to lose, their wings:
they start to lose the very strings
of sound itself. Give up the skies:
you're left your weight. And your last ties
to anything that sings.

Yet Not to Listen to That Sung Nothing

I woke in Florida, late and lazy, my sill
(my few flown hours from winter) a blaze
of tropic, and on it, like a small soul
spilling its echoes of heaven—a fluff of bliss
in full throb—a mockingbird went on and on
in the thrill of itself to itself in that near sun.

Birds have nothing to say. Yet not to listen
to that sung nothing is the death of rapture.
Rapture or loneliness? —the difference is in
what one is reminded of, listening. Only after
reminders can one hear the first, last, and first
again sweet scald of nothing in the bird-burst

godlings that wake, like rose-heads trembling
on their trellises, or hibiscus like a million
butterflies just lighting, or the rambling
trumpets of a vine lifting to blow to Zion
that the time is come of the splitting of the horn
of plenty, that the bird-burst sun is born,

and not heaven, nor earth, nor any waking man
can hold the outpouring of an instant
of nothing, all, and nothing, again and again
on its sill in that sun, where the infant
soul of a bird, its few flown hours
from winter again, sings, and a man, wakened, hears.

Gulls Land and Cease to Be

Spread back across the air, wings wide,
    legs out, the wind delicately
dumped in balance, the gulls ride
    down, down, hang, and exactly
touch, folding not quite at once
    into their gangling weight, but
taking one step, two, wings still askance,
    reluctantly, at last, shut,
      twitch one look around
      and are aground.

At First Flower of the Easy Day

At first flower of the easy day
a buck went wading through the mist.
Legless, he seemed to sail away.
A brown swan with a mythic twist
of antlers to his changeling head.
All that the weaving Greeks referred
to plastic nature's shifting thread

he evidenced. I saw him turn
and dip his head into that pond
and flash the white flag at his stern,
then lift his head and sail beyond
an isle of spruces to the right.
What do we ask of any wraith
but the Greek fact in its first light

that makes of morning's beasts the day
our nights would dream if they knew how?
Starting from this dawn, I could say
sad Io's name to any cow
and have her eyes confirm my guess.
Unless her farmer came like Zeus
and waved me off the premises.

Bees and Morning Glories

Morning glories, pale as a mist drying,
fade from the heat of the day, but already
hunchback bees in pirate pants and with peg-leg
hooks have found and are boarding them.

This could do for the sack of the imaginary
fleet. The raiders loot the galleons even as they
one by one vanish and leave still real
only what has been snatched out of the spell.

I've never seen bees more purposeful except
when the hive is threatened. They know
the good of it must be grabbed and hauled
before the whole feast wisps off.

They swarm in light and, fast, dive in,
then drone out, slow, their pantaloons heavy
with gold and sunlight. The line of them,
like thin smoke, wafts over the hedge.

And back again to find the fleet gone.
Well, they got this day's good of it. Off
they cruise to what stays open longer.
Nothing green gives honey. And by now

you'd have to look twice to see more than green
where all those white sails trembled
when the world was misty and open
and the prize was there to be taken.

One Morning

I remember my littlest one in a field
running so hard at the morning in him
he kicked the heads off daisies. Oh, wild
and windy and spilling over the brim
of his sun-up juices he ran
in the dew of himself. My son.

And the white flower heads
shot like sparks where his knees
pumped, and his hot-shod
feet took off from time, as who knows
when ever again a running morning will be
so light-struck, flower-sparked-full between him and me.

There's this to a good day's sweat
high in the branches trimming and down
into the ground rooting—I'm not used to it
any more but it reminds me when I'm done
and sprawl shaky with tiredness, wet
in the sun's wringer. Sweat tells me again
who my people were. And yes, there's more
to it. But without sweat I wouldn't want
it. It takes the whole body to be sure
of what you're remembering. I can't
say my father's or my grandfather's name
a better way than this sog-tired numb
joy of having touched green growing
and the dirt under it and the day going.

Even then I can't really touch them. Not ever
again. They had first things and the power
and the ignorance that go to the receiver
of first things only; that and no more.

I've lost it. I'm my own first. There was never
a man of my blood before
who spoke more than one tougue, or *that*
in a way courts wouldn't laugh at.
My father did read some. But it was
his mountain he came from, not the mind
of man. He had ritual, not ideas. His

world that I cannot find
except as my body aches and sweats hewing,
was holy and dim. But doing
his work, I rest. I remember this:
it is good to be able. To hold axe and saw
and do first things again. I miss
this the desked days I go. I see
him here. I know him. But he is
more than I can teach my children. They
have no first life. *That* is their loss.
I wish we were Jews and could say
the names of what made us.
I could weep by slow waters for my son
who has no history, no name
he knows long, no ritual from which he came,
and no fathers but the forgotten.

He who could sweat down, tree by tree,
a whole wood and touch no memory.

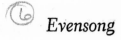

In late afternoon, when the light
no longer has a source, but is brushed
like a glowing powder onto leaves
and housefronts, a cock cardinal
in the sconce of a dead treetop
flickers like a wick, and calls his hen
to roost. Or simply calls.
On a wire spanning my lawn
from maples to blue spruce, a dove
repeats its slow broken sound
for some minutes of this world,
then leaves it. One by one
the bright dusts wear off. Trees
and sky enlarge toward one another,
mass into one shadow.

The ardor of this world looked at
in the moving meaninglessness
of light and of the lives
that sing to it, and leave,
is, finally, the grace there is.

Birds, Like Thoughts

Watch a wild turkey come in to land—
(they are rare, but a man can find most
of what he wants if he wants it enough
to look for it) —you see a long slant
out of the air, like the approach of
some queer plane. Its landing gear first
let down, then agitated, it starts to run
before it touches, finishes yards on
from the point of touch down; and only then
folds its wings and is back, a hen again.

Not wrens, warblers, swallows— (I can't even see
what it is swallows do on the air. They
change it, exceed it, make it serve impossibility)—
all smaller (not lesser) birds play
instantly in and out of the air. There are no
parts to their coming, going. A whirl and they light;
a whirl, and they are airborne. Watch a jay go
its long dart through branches. It is too right
to need caution. It lands like an arrow
with no separation of its motions— So!

And there it is, and instantly gone if it feels
like it. Talk about landing on a dime!—
it could land on the edge of one. I've watched
every bird I could find to look at as it wheels,
heaves, whirls, glides. Whatever is hatched
to wings has its own way with them. But I'm
sure of one thing: the more weight you take to air,
the more space you need to get down
the more slowly. Birds are like thoughts: they're
more instant as they stay light. Both come and gone.

Sea Marshes in Winter

Marsh hummocks that were a sabbath hill
for a witches' dance of lives the last weather I looked,
go Christian as Calvary in the stone still
and sackcloth sky. At four, a wind-hooked
glacier of cloud chills a last thought and the snow
starts. And all that night that comes at once
the snow sifts dry as salt, scratching the window.
Then day leaks back from the edge. A half-light hunts
somewhere to settle, a place to begin, but slumps
onto the black-streaked sheet and the dead white humps
between me and the sea. It never quite—
not all that day—makes up to enough light
to see a world by. And still I look at this
world as world's will be seen—in what light there is.

Aquarium

There is almost no such fish as this which is
the children's awe for a minute, and the world's
glassed from the world. It was another imagination
than anyone's that colored it with minerals
and hung it trembling from the rubber pouch
of its own hanging mouth as from a perfect balance:
the weight of the sac behind it precisely equal
      the weight of the world before it.

A self, I think. Shaped gross and delicate
to its million years of currents out of sight.
A frown like a tragic mask's but drawn in pink
cordage and mottled black. A pig-iron body
the shape of bloat, yet trembling weightless as
burst milkweed. A fantail
drawn from a Chinese dream of fires dancing.
      It is one thing of this world.

What world is there but the world looked at?
I see and am seen. Until all seeing blinds
in the idiot-certain hang of this in-taking, all-taking,
and impossible brine mouth dry children gawk at
by permission of the City of New York
whose glass walls split the world into time and Sunday.
Two utter imaginations at their meeting.
      Seeing and being seen.

Old Man

When the old man who had bought all his wives
ran out of cash, he took to feeding pigeons
in Washington Square. He had never learned
how to summon a meeting except by a bribe.
Now he was down to peanuts. But for once
he was buying responses that really
came to him and then really flew. He hummed
in that cloud, and wished he might scatter
diamonds to his pigeons as he had once to his
various chicks. Luckily for the pigeons,
however, he was beyond diamonds and could strew
only what was useful—a difference that made
the difference, for he grew gentle in the wing-worked
sun about him and learned he would die a lover.

When a Man Dies

When a man dies angels tick.
An alarm of roses rings.
Folded moths on every wick
crack like fine glass, and their wings
slide like powder down the light.
So goodmorning. So goodnight.

Where the pane breaks rain will fall.
Every house turns inside out.
God's the root that tangles all.
What the devil is about
I don't know and I don't care.
But anyone can hear the air

hissing from the things we say
when we stand beside the bed
as the dead man starts away
from the rooftree overhead
to the seepage underfoot.
Where else shall we think to put

Dad and Mother in their time?
Deeper than the judgment waits
beetles click what churches chime.
Eternities of figure-eights
scribble out the face that was
the instant that it leaves the house.

So goodmorning. So goodnight.
So goodlife—if it *was* good.
May great roses ring me bright
my last instant understood
when I hear the air hiss out
of—whatever it was about.

From Adam's Diary

In the planetarium of an apple tree
I shook some spiral nebulae
and sent some systems reeling, just to see
how that might be. Just between time and me,
to see how it might be
to shake a universe—or an apple tree—
and see what fell, and think how it would be
if any of what fell was me.
None of it was—that day. But I could see
it all would be. Some day. Whatever tree.

Two Hours

I. EVENING

The low-fi scrapes the phrases from the strings
of something neither of us was listening to.
Whatever it is, the strings grate still, the drums
begin to cough a bronchial bass crack. You,
I, someone, thought a music, but it comes
wrong from the machine. Which brings

me to you-and-me as you start to undress
at last (which brings me to you) and how
frothily from foam-trim perkily your thighs
dimple and your arms reach and grow
till they are elements of the light and the wise
S's of your hips enter the great S
of your languor as, reaching behind,
you unstrap and unribbon and your breasts
go from the advertised to the invincible
first line of mantime, and a last rustle rests
you ungirdled at the bird-sung well
of gardens this twisted music cannot find,

of lights and airs and palpable here-and-now
to confound all Heaven's recorders and amplifiers.
How shall they hear us on any machine of theirs?
—your nakedness is more music than they have wires.
Yet, if it's true that angels watch in pairs,
they still may learn. Come here. We'll *show* them how.

II. MORNING

A morning of the life there is
in the house beginning again
its clutters in the sun

babbles and sways and tells
time from its sailing cribs. Enter
three pirate energies to murder sleep:

the bed rocks with their boarding:
a fusilade of blather
sweeps the white decks. We're taken!

—Goodmorning, sweet with chains.
We win all but the fight.
Do as they say—I'll meet you here tonight.

Of Fish and Fishermen

Fish are subtle. Fishermen
are gross and stinking and they lurch
hauling their nets. Which clod of them
could shimmer like a cod or perch
through blue and green and purple spells?
It isn't shimmering grace that tells
in the long run. It's being taught
to track and set and haul and stink.
If stinking's part of it. It's not?
It needn't be? That's what you think.

An Aspect of the Air

Through my hemlocks and the spruce beyond,
mist hangs and closes. What change is this?
Not a bird dares it. Not so much as a frond
stirs in the shadowless absence
of this light I see by, not knowing what I see,
there in the green caves and up into a sky
that isn't there, except as there must be
some source for any light. I don't see, I
conjecture sources. It is too still
not to be thinking out from things, not to feel
a presence of the unreality that *will*
mystify what incloses us. Mist is not real;
not by the handful. And thought is not
fact, nor measurable. It is simply there.
An inclosing condition. A dimension taught
the sourceless light. An aspect of the air.

PERSON TO PERSON

"Eyum die-ah-leen that num-ber," sings the voice we all know
from fate, taped crisply out of this life, yet blurred, too;
   much as an over-used die goes on stamping parts
with its worn intaglios. What it shapes almost fits, will do,

will have to do. We have the way we all live. It starts
crisp and wears. Yet, I could be some sweetheart's
   hope about to say it all. I could be man's own last word
waiting to be gasped. I could be the weather reports

on which everyone's picnic depends. And she, the half-occurred
body from which the voice repeats (if what we have heard
   is possibly a sound from a body in which anyone
lives) might as readily be swiveled to the switchboard

of Heaven, melodious to this world's need, plugging in
tears, prayers, and praises, each to its office. Routine
   and eternity must have the commonness of their sound
in common. What need can there be to imagine

what repeats itself endlessly? —She *does* dial. The round
whirr of distance grows on the wire. Like the ground
   whine of insect legs, the phone burrs. Stops. Burrs again.
"Eyum ring-een," the insect says. I die bound

to my wheel of patience, broken because I want, drawn
bone from bone by the nothing happening of it. "No one
   see-ums to ants-err." —Strange the idioms in which this
non-death is told. I can reach no one. "Thank you," I say, gone

under the ether of failure. Not dead, no. But missing and amiss.

Citation

This decent executive person is
saying to me heartily to the economy
magnetically and to the casualties
here and hereabout incomprehensibly

Nothing. He produces better plywood more than, expands his business
very, and often conscientiously
serves whenever his country, his

community, his wife, faithfully always,
to his kids hail-fellowing, a pal, and
to his basement workshop at day's
end goes hobbily happy to cut and sand

precisions he knows all about. He could,
his wife girlie-giggles, almost make
a world (were worlds made of plywood)
showing me whatnots and a break-

front and the slidingest concealed bar
in the rumpus room. And I, for one,
can testify that my assets are
much fat-folded since this good person

let me in on the ground floor of this
many-mansioned house whose towers
he has no cause to doubt, in whose
cellar he has never—horrors!—

thought to dig, nor of the deed read
more than his self-evidently enough-
signature, nor in his head
asked any foolish questions of.

Language ends in the tongue's clay pit.
Say the name of the dead man: he is not there.
Say the name of the dead poet: who hears it?
My friend and teacher, John Holmes, who made air
answer to the words of his name is dead
of everything he knew, understood, said,

and made sayable. A variation of what he was.
A stubborn and a weak man—then, quietly, that hour
of his language forming, a poet, a place of pause
for the thought, the thing, that came and was sure.
He died in agonies his life was too calm to have thought,
yet terrible enough, yet not

too terrible to unform his same mixed self while he had
strength enough to say it. Pain
is the other clay pit, the gray-yellow bad
water that gathers. Life is the rain
that will not stay clean. Language, the wind
that brings all thought to mind.

Pain washed him dirty, made of him the stale
pool original water comes to. The wind
that brought him is over. I loved him. Failed him. Fail
him now, and will, and fail myself. Till we find
failures to love from there will be no
love. His tongueless ruin, mine, go

to one another. Is there more language
than the chiming of our losses? It ends.
This language, and any, ends. What good is rage?
a literary tradition. We were friends

and are not. Barring wreckage of car, plane, train,
and such chances, I think much the same drain

will soil me past words. He lets me dare
say nothing. As all is said. These lines talk
round the clay places. They do not care
to be memorable. We are not. We walk
what health says us, and die used
as run-rain. The silt in us, loosed,

silts out. But the water never clears.
Not wholly. And words are not understood;
they live beyond understanding. What years
language stays to me I shall sing the good
of language that has no cause to mean.
I shall say his name among many—John Holmes—and a clean

rain will seem possible. The best of a man
is what he thought of and could not be.
The best of the rest, what he said, what we all can
say, or think of saying, because we see
the clay-gray gathering of all water, but drink
from what first wells our most thoughts think.

My Father Died Imperfect as a Man

My father died imperfect as a man.
My mother lied him to perfections. I
knew nothing, and had to guess we all mean
our lives in honor of the most possible lie.

She was no more herself than a gull is
its own idea to make on any air
precisions of itself. What instinct does
for the egg in nature, history did for her.

So Italy's dark duplicating spines
bred her precisely herself, instinctual as
peasantry breeds in any Apennines.
Those centuries repeat; they do not pass.

And everywhere at their end which is always again,
always present, and everywhere the same—
as alike as gulls, as grass, bred of the chain
that breeds its likeness back through any name,

the ritual women sweep their Italies,
move step by step from grave to birth to grave,
scrub clothes and speak to God on the same knees,
and take exactly the shape of how they live.

So history lied my father from his death,
she having no history that would let him be
imperfect and worth keeping vigils with.
She made a saint of him. And she made me

kneel to him every night. When I was bad,
he shadowed me. And always knew my lies.

I was too young to know him, but my bed
lay under him and God, and both their eyes

bored through the dark to damn me as I was,
imperfect as a boy and growing worse.
Somehow I loved her in that haunted house
she made of her own flesh. And so, in course,

forgave myself and learned how to forgive.
Love must intend realities. I can
be anything but saintly and still live
my father's love, imperfect as a man.

I Remember the House That Was

I remember the terraces down from Portland Road
to the Shrewsbury River, and the lyre-shaped gray
tulip tree trunks above, and the holly below
the house where Fletcher Pratt lived. I don't know
who lives there now. A doctor, I've heard say,
who raises Great Danes, some of which have showed.

Well, I myself have bought a dead man's house
and live in it. A nameplate on the door
becomes a calendar. A letter sent
comes back unknown. Perhaps a doggy scent
clings to it. Probably not. But truth is more
imaginable than proven. Fletcher was

the keeper of great doorways. When he died
some part of all doors warped—imagined doors.
What we call real of real estate still stood.
Was salable. Was sold. But if the wood
stayed to the house's sills and steps and floors
the house went from itself, its walls blown wide,

its unconveyable entrances all shut,
or gaping in on nothing. Doors must lead
to presences. Walls must be built around.
They still are, I suppose. Someone has found
and bought a house he likes. And Fletcher, dead,
is out of tenancy. And that's about

the gist of it. The trees and terraces
still ride to the Atlantic, and the sun
rises from water in a doubled blaze
to what was Fletcher's great house those salt days
and windy gabled nights when everyone
was at the party in the house that was.

An Afternoon in the Park

I lived an age that could not be.
Formal and fast to every look
its men stood to each other's eye,
signed in each other's common book.

Nothing but men had changed in this.
Birds were exactly birds. The sea
kept every fold just as it is
in what must pass for memory.

The lion dozing in the zoo
of that grave Helicon looked out
as much like Zeus as lions do
in any Bronx. It was about

three-thirty of an afternoon
I got that world into my thought.
Would four o'clock have been too soon
to start back from it? I had not

meant to come back at all. But then
some worlds are good enough to mean,
some only good enough for men.
And, yes, I knew which I had seen.

Reality and Willie Yeats

Reality and Yeats were two.
He even told it what to do—
where to enter, what to say,
and when to turn and go away
and let the ectoplasms take
his hand and write. And, writing, make
realities Reality
could not outstare. At least not while
he held it in the trance of style.

There the style is—speech and song.
Long as Reality is long.
It is the stylist lost his tongue,
and lost his texture and his tone,
and vapored off. Now, skin and bone,
styleless as mud caked into stone,
Reality and Yeats are one.

*　　*　　*

Mme. Blavatsky, who was part
of Willie's vapors (not his art),
arranged with friends before she died
sure signals from the Other Side.
Some of her friends insist she tried
to send them back but none came through.
That same Reality you and you
(and I) are never sure of, must
(I conclude) include such dust
as chokes off signals. What we hear
is: poets die, their poems appear
still to transmit, and still to be
signals from some Reality.

Instances

Walt Whitman took the Earth to bed.
Insatiate man! He felt her stir
and advertised it as a love.
She let him. And by reason of
the unadvertised, when he was dead
she took him back to bed with her.

Millay, too, did her best to take
the whole thing in her arms. Her reach
fell short, and so she sang of that.
Sometimes she sang a little flat.
More usually her voice would break
and her high-C come out a screech.

Emily as a general thing
kept things to scale. At least by day.
In wild nights she was harder pressed.
Not the whole moon clutched to her breast
could stay her. May our late thanks bring
this lady gardens that *will* stay.

Poets are mad. Perhaps the act
of singing addles any brain.
Perhaps the best of anything
is wanting it enough to sing
the madness up from any fact.
Poets are mad. Are bankers sane?

A dog with a tin can tied to its tail is
no philosopher but could yet, if only in
longest time to never quite, be learning
there are more attachments to love than ever
puppies reckon when they take their first God
by mistake, wriggling—oh don't they wriggle! —their
tails, rumps, legs, and everything to lick the manhand,
Love, that anytime becomes the hand that ties.

Poor dim parishioners of no church at all!
I don't much care for love that sells itself to
tameness, crawling back to lick the hand that did
it. Yes, dogs and boys make out their two parts
of one damp valentine, but a man needs to see wild
things running, sure of their fear of the manscent,
the scar it makes on the first air of creatures, keeping
themselves themselves, wary and fast. A fox, I think,
is a dog that learned about mankind and lived.

A Blaze for Everything and Everything in Its Blaze

Once of a world I never knew
I flexed a muscle big as a lie.
Hayfoot, Strawfoot, one and two,
some were pulling down the sky,
some were stomping off to town,
and some took off and never came down,

> singing: *The navy gave the baby gravy.*
> *Graves Registration gave it meat.*
> *The Catholic chaplain said an Ave.*
> *Its mother was smoking in the street.*
> *Its father was smoldering in lime.*
> *A charming army of bonhomie*
> *sang in a classic rape of rhyme*
> *of the homely girl with parts so homey*
> *she humped a squadron at a time.*

Once of a dream in a world that lay
Hayfoot in and Strawfoot out,
the last Inspector drove away:
we dumped twelve thousand rounds and put
whiskey in the ammo cans
to prove we were Americans,

> singing: *The corps put up a score of corpses.*
> *Someone or other picked the hill.*
> *The forces cursed the horses' arses.*
> *No one was very hard to kill.*
> *(Some were a little hard to find.)*
> *Parts of starlets toured the ramparts*
> *with a stack in front and a stack behind.*
> *The King and Queen sent tea and crumpets.*
> *God (and the President) spoke His mind.*

All in a roar at the world's dawn edge
we revved our motors, we said goodbye—
a pleasure, sir, and a privilege.
Thank you, madam: if I should die,
there is some breeze from every death
that is forever bourbon on my breath,

    singing: *The navy gave the baby gravy,* etc.

All in a huff of a world away
a hulk of wind came barging through.
A luffing voice began to say,
"The world is sick of precisely you."
—over and over and up and down
every corpse in the bombed out town,

    singing: *The corps put up a score of corpses,* etc.

Out of a noon of a gull-shot shore,
Hayfoot in and Strawfoot out
of a puddle of sea at the edge of war,
I watched the white birds wheel about
the sea-sweet bounteous bloats that rise,
the pearls of heaven in their eyes,

    singing: *The navy gave the baby gravy,* etc.

All of a dream of a world of bliss,
I watched the feasts of Heaven start.
The white birds flutter when they kiss.
They fan us to the very heart.
Sunlit blazings wheel and drip,
torn from the stiff upper lip,

    singing: *The corps put up a score of corpses,* etc.

Lines

I did not have exactly a way of life
but the bee amazed me and the wind's plenty
was almost believable. Hearing a magpie laugh

through a ghost town in Wyoming, saying Hello
in Cambridge, eating cheese by the frothy Rhine,
leaning from plexiglass over Tokyo,

I was not able to make one life of all
the presences I haunted. Still the bee
amazed me, and I did not care to call

accounts from the wind. Once only, at Pompeii,
I fell into a sleep I understood,
and woke to find I had not lost my way.

SOUL TO BODY

That affable, vital, inspired even, and well-paid
    persuader of sensibility with the witty asides
but, at core, lucent and unswayed—
    a gem of serenest ray—besides
  being the well-known poet, critic, editor, and middle-high
  aesthete of the circuit is, alas, I.

Some weep for him: a waster of talent. Some
    snicker at the thought of talent in him. He leaves
in a Cadillac, has his home away from home
    where the dolls are, and likes it. What weaves
  vine leaves in the hair weaves no laurel for the head.
  The greedy pig, he might as well be dead—

to art at least—for wanting it all and more—
    cash, bourbon, his whim away from whom.
He's a belly, a wallet, a suit, a no-score
    of the soul. Sure, he looks like a boom
  coming, but whatever he comes to, sits to, tries
  to sit still to and say, is a bust. It's booby prize

time at the last dance whenever he
    lets a silence into himself. It grinds
against the jitter in him and dies. Poetry
    is what he gabs at, then dabbles in when he finds
  hobby time for it between serious pitches
  for cash, free-loading, and the more expensive bitches.

I give him up, say I. (And so say I.)
    There are no tears in him. If he does feel,

he's busier at Chateaubriand than at asking why.
      He lives the way he lives as if it were real.
   A con man. A half truth. A swindler in the clear.
   Look at him guzzle. He actually likes it here!

BODY TO SOUL

That grave, secretive, aspirant even, and bang-kneed
      eternalist of boneyards with the swallowed tongue
but, at dream source, flaming and fire-freed—
      a monk of dark-celled rays—along
   with being heretic, ignorant, Jesuit, and who-
   knows-what skeleton, is, alas, not wholly you.

I've watched you: a scratcher of scabs that are not
      there. An ectoplasmic jitter. Who was it spent
those twenty years and more in the polyglot
      of nightmares talking to Pa? If I went
   over your head to God, it *was* over your head.
   Whose butt grew stiff in the chair the nights you read

whose eyes blind and wrote whose nerves to a dither?
      And who got up in the cold to revise you by light?
You're a glowworm. A spook. A half-strung zither
      with a warped sounding box: you pluck all right
   but if what whines out is music, an alley cat
   in moon-heat on a trashcan is Kirsten Flagstadt.

Yes, I like it here. Make it twenty times worse
      and I'd still do it over again, even with you
like a monkey on my back. You dried-out wet-nurse,
      think you're the poet, do you? You're wind that blew

on ashes that wouldn't catch. You were gone
the instant I learned the poem is belly and bone.

I gave *you* up. Like a burp. For a better weather
    inside my guts. And, *yes*, I want it all—
grab, gaggle, and rut—as sure as death's no breather.
    Though you wouldn't know, being dead as yesterday's squall
where the sea's a diamond-spilling toss in the bright brace
of today's air, to glitter me time and place.

Summer Morning with Sun and Showers

A gloss-green morning comes deep to my window.
Rain purls small as the grasshoppers of my clock
whose horn legs strum the hours to song. I laze
hazy to crickety time fiddling sun and shower.

But the ants are there, too. In silent safaris
over the singsong dial their feelers
roll the minutes, like crumbs, away
from song to the colonial burrows under rain-
gloss, sun-wash, leaf-wag, and all my lazy first
float in the green letters writing my window full.
—These two orders to wake to. And which, they ask,
shall I answer? —time's voice or silence? (I yawn.)

Well, then, whatever goes, and as it goes.
Sing up. Put down. Time tells and will not be told.
Grasshoppers, be my pleasure. Ants, provide.
Morning, begin. I have no worlds to change.

What Was Her Name?

Someone must make out the cards
for the funeral of the filing clerk.
Poor bony rack with her buzzard's
jowled eyes bare as a dirk
and as sharp for dead fact, she
could have done it better than anyone
will do it for her. It will be,
to be sure, done.
And the flowers sent. And the office closed
for the half day it takes
for whatever we are supposed
to make of the difference it makes
to file the filing clerk
where we can forget her.

Someone will do the work
she used to do better.

On Flunking a Nice Boy Out of School

I wish I could teach you how ugly
decency and humility can be when they are not
the election of a contained mind but only
the defenses of an incompetent. Were you taught
meekness as a weapon? Or did you discover,
by chance maybe, that it worked on mother
and was generally a good thing—
at least when all else failed—to get you over
the worst of what was coming. Is that why you bring
these sheepfaces to Tuesday?
                              They won't do.
It's three months work I want, and I'd sooner have it
from the brassiest lumpkin in pimpledom, but have it,
than all these martyred repentances from you.

To No End Ever

The pretty ones have their problems; the plain ones,
themselves, and it is not enough. It *is*
a vanity, and if not sinful (as once
it was schoolmarmed to be) still amiss
(because a shallowing of oneself) to make love
to a mirror. (Where can you go when you leave?)

But what is it to see there what it hurts
to look at, from, like? to be a girl in
no body worth wanting? It's worse
than vanity, surely. It's the kind of sin
you fall into without being guilty, and can't hide
from anyone, yourself least. I could have cried

for the sad bump of a thing in my poetry class
who sat in my office, all a-scraggle, and said
"Supposing I did do more work and did pass—
what would I pass to?" Like a fathead
I quoted Yeats out of the textbook
on hearts being earned. She gave me a look

with no end to it ever and said, "Being me
is like driving a truck to a sports-car rally—except
that I can't get out of it." I gave her C.
She was a C for life and would have to accept—
and couldn't—not gracefully—what was hers to take.
Not luck. Not mercy. Nothing a wish would make.

Autobiography of a Comedian

Years long in the insanities of adolescence—
because my father had died but still
spoke to me, because my mother was mad,
because the cross was bloody on the One Hill—

I wrestled God gaunt on my knees and wet
in the sizzle of nightmare wakings till
there was nothing to do but die or embrace
a more comic spirit. Which, being hard to kill,

I did. I told jokes my family fled from.
My friends knew me through cracks in the door.
Father Ryan black-sheeped me from the pulpit.
—God knows he had more than enough to deplore.

Then suddenly my jokes became lucrative.
My wallet acquired a vocabulary. My four
thumbs and twelve toes turned jugglers.
I learned to dance loose. And the more

I shuffled the more money, cars, houses
I got for it. I grew rich grinning.
Bankers learned to pronounce my name.
I even won at Harold's Club. I'm still winning

what I have no real use for but
might as well take. In my beginning
was no end of a wry humor. I am my broker's
keeper. Not even my hair is thinning.

I tell you this world's as crazy as I was once.
Even scholars take me seriously. And why

complain, you say? Friend, I am trying
as simple and as marvelous a thing as honesty.

As I might say I love my wife, enjoy
playing with my children, expect to die
and not to profit by the experience—
I think we are of some Stone Age, you and I.

How do we make sense of ourselves?
I do not understand presidents, popes, kings,
ministers, marshals, or policemen
except as I see the ritual featherings

of the tribes in their hair. What do I know
of the invisible people I killed for wings
when I was a gunner for our tribe?
I remember the fires we started, not the things

we burned in them. I think Harold,
crazy as he is for God now, has our real
mystery in his spinning department store.
What we all pray to is the dice, the wheel,

and the holy jackpot. Have you *seen*
the grandmothers praying at those steel
altars where the heaven-eyes blink and wink
fruit, bells, and dominion? It's God they feel

coming at the next click. But Harold
keeps the books for his three per cent. Another
comic spirit, except that he believes it
and works at it. As once my grandmother

in *her* tribe's dark, kept herbs and spells
and studied signs and dreams. Why bother
to believe what there is a sure three per cent of?
Somehow we must keep our brother.

by what will not be kept. Between
our slapstick successes and our wry
confessions, there is the day the sun starts.
The low sea to the west of Reno and the high

desert to the east. This world. And in it
the mercy that sees and knows why
we must not love ourselves too much—
though, having no other, we must, somehow, try.

I. As I hear the family thinking it

This is the body of my good gray practical dead
uncle. We are going to bury it today. We are
not going to bury it because it is good gray
or practical, but because it is dead. We are
observing, I submit, the proper proprieties.

Were he good gray practical and not dead, we
certainly would not bury him. Not today.
We would let him go on burying himself in
his good gray practical way. It is because
he can no longer bury himself that we

do it for him. We are a family and we observe
our observances. We have even chosen a
good gray practical day. For, more or less
inevitably, he is dead, and we know how to
put two and two together and get it all

buried. What else is a family for? Do you think
we would let our uncle bury himself all
these years and not finish the job for him?
Besides, he is unusably dead. Which, even
as a matter of practicality, changes things:

What good would it do to keep him? He
could only grow more noticeable than
we have ever allowed him to be, or than
would entirely fit his character, or
what we took to be his character, what

the bottle had left of it. He did try us. But
he is dead. This is his body under a good

gray sky with all the practical arrangements
arranged. And the family here, practically mourning.
But a family. And one that knows what to do.

II. As I find myself remembering

But because he bought me my first puppy (a brownsilk
ears nose and tail all going with a red ribbon
around its neck) and gave me (on another birthday) my
first .22 (with which I walked whole continents any
afternoon) I don't care what rumpot he bloated into
and floated out of mushy. He is dead. As dead
as if he had turned into a magnolia and decayed
open. But by all the sick flowers of this world,
I remember a gorgeous and a boozy man with
hairy arms and neat hands and an eye that never
missed a quail or a pheasant (as I believe my dream).
And because he was made to hide even his ruin, I kiss
his stone forehead and leave him my tear openly, for
myself, perhaps, but openly—who was a dream I had
young and lived glad in. I did him no good ever
and I am ashamed to remember how he could laugh once.

Salt Lake City

There was a roof just under my hotel window
and a squat pyramidal skylight covered with netting.
On the netting lay two dead pigeons:
a slate-colored one on the upper right slope
and a white one just below the center.
To the left, over the old bricks and the new fronts
of Main Street, the mountains rose forever,
snow covered and coruscating in the sun.

I had checked in that Monday night when there was
nothing to see. Tuesday morning when I opened the blinds
there were mountains, Main Street, and the dead pigeons.
Nothing happened to any of them. When I checked out
for the airport on Saturday only the week was gone.
And not in a straight line, but as if it had been glued
to a revolving drum to begin again exactly
where it ended. I was fearless and would have stayed

out of no more than curiosity. Had I stayed,
there was a chance I might never have fought free
of the drum. I might have been glued to it as to flypaper
all one revolving eternity that would immediately start over.
There is some danger in anything. Generally, however,
courage is superfluous to eternity and fear irrelevant.
I would have stayed but it happened I was busy—
meaning I had some money to make in Chicago.

Sequence

In big country, out there where the land
is all shoulders and the enormous
is the least unit of the eye's map, in sand-
and-gravel genesis tilting to the Navaho's
cloudy ghost on the bald peaks above pine,
above the canyon paradise of waterfalls
and grass-combed waters, where totems whine
in the wind, and a church of bird-calls
repeats itself empty, and the sky slants
like a glacier from space
                    —to nothing now,
and no history, of all that first silence
hunters and chiefs laid their bones to,
sure of what land it was, and eternally
                         —there,
watching the waitress lean down (a honey),
I lounged in a heated pool on a raft of air,
and took the bourbon she passed me, tinkling like money.

Helmeted, booted, numbered, horsed, and always at a distance,
the polo players mill, fumble, jostle, and one at last clicks
the white ball far on its high arc while six knot up behind
and one in an epic lunge chases the white curve to hit or miss
the nothing between two uprights. He is, of course, pursued
by the giant that is always there to oppose giants, and who
    means
to deflect the diagram his way, spinning the arc back through
the pack, and beyond, and to click it home to his own nothing
between the uprights at the other end of the world.
                        So
from pole to pole they go, Greeks and Trojans, identical
to the end and great in their distances, their seven-and-a-half
minutes at a time and six times over till the last diagram
has been risked, the falls taken, the horses lathered, replaced,
and lathered again, and the crowd, forever small in its distance,
has applauded again and again like wind rattling the dry trees
of a hill beyond.
                Then, breathing hard, they walk their horses
to the grooms, station wagons, and trailers that wait
to pack distances close and take them expensively to rest
between glories; and the players, dismounted, with towels
around their necks and their hair sweat-curled, light cigarettes
and are no longer giants in the dusty world the cars leave
for their home beyond heroes; till only the field is left,
like an emptied world, its grasses charged by great shadows.

Coq au Vin

In Paris once, just as the waiter
in his priesthood laid before me
a silver-capped ritual steam
which he uncovered in the certainty
of the body and the blood and the
fragrance of attended art, summoning
me as his parishioner to bend
my head into the steam and inhale
the holiness of his intention—and as
I did bow in homage to his office
(hearing God say, "Qu'est-ce que tu fais?"
to which I replied, "Je m'amuse") —just
then, through the sacred vapors
of our toy altar, I saw black before me
the unuttered scream of a ruined presence.

It was a woman. Or not a woman. A
residue that was to the idea of woman
what excretion was to my priest's
holy viand—an animated rot
of the flesh, a face gnawed by syphilis,
eyes webbed red in their filthy gashes,
a nose grated like the Sphinx's
but to blood, a mouth like a spoiled
fruit. She stood gibbering and
cursing. A beggar, but too sure of her
horror to need beg. She accused.
Destroying us with her reality. Her
ruin gloating at us.
     I emptied
my pockets blindly and bowed to her
cursing. I would have stripped

and given her my clothes and the
hair of my body had not the waiter
and the owner and the owner's wife
rushed her, herding her, not daring
to touch, parsing small money into
her cupped claw as she stalked, still
gibbering and cursing, back into
whatever unmentionable hole she had
come from like pus to infect our
novena of sauces in the stinking
abbey of God-the-Tourist, who said
in Midwestern, "Living it up, son?"

And I flung down my napkin and fled
with a sound in me like ripped cloth.

The Mountain Lent

The trains in that country
sent black roses to heaven
from the snow sides of the air
and the avalanche-ridden
rafters of the world.
Men roped together
climbed like a German music against the sky.
A sunburst bloodied their footholds in the weather.

"It is the rescue party," said the conductor.
"They go to rescue the corpses from the snow.
Always they go and it is always corpses,
their faces gray as pigeons from the cold.
Ever? Perhaps. Perhaps even this time.
Tomorrow or the next day we will know.
The trains cannot leave. There is no hurry."

We sat in that country
on the glass cliffs of the air
with brandy and coffee
by the scar of the avalanche
like a scuff in the sky
below and above us,
till the men, still roped together, descended
like angels in bearskins, and dead of their own weight.

"They have had to leave them," said the Yugoslav.
"God knows, they will keep till spring," said the Sicilian.
"Listen, the church bells," said the Scandinavian.
"They could not ring before," said the stationmaster,
"for fear of starting the slides. When a party leaves
the church trembles all night with the prayers of women
but the bells are tied. It is the mountain Lent."

A Sentiment for December 25

Caught as we all are in the human condition—
Subject to vices variously begun—
in curiosity, from nature, of malaise.
Hungry for joy and fed less than our hunger.
Charitable when we can save ourselves
from more involvement than we know how to bear.
Simple in our silences, made intricate by vocabularies.
Greedy because we were all once children.
Forgoing because we have read dreams and visions
that do not come to us when we lay the book by.
Loving in desperation, in fear of loneliness.
Begetting in the arsons and Olympics of first love
or in the habituated rutting of the long bed
the children that sadden us to an uneasy tolerance.
Afraid of death in our dying and liberated
only partially by the partial loss of ignorance.
Eager for friendships from which we may demand
what we ourselves give with two motives, if at all.
Suspected by States for our best intuitions.
Solemn at funerals but glad to have outlived
one other as proof that we are, after all, right.
Liars because we must live in what seems possible.
Fools because we lie, and fools again for assuming
the possible to be any more likely than the impossible.
Faithless because our houses are destroyable but not our fears.
Brave because we dare not stop to think. Proud
because we are wrong. Wrathful because we are powerless.
Envious because we are uncertain. Lazy because we were born.
Avaracious because we are afraid. Gluttonous
because bellies are a mother to warm and assure us.
Murderous and adulterous because opportunity and energy
will sometimes be added to motive. Ungrateful
because gratitude is a debt, and because it is easier
to betray our benefactors than to await new benefactions.
Religious because it is dark at night, and because

we have been instructed, and because it is easier to obey
than to believe our senses or to learn to doubt them
exhaustively. Sad because we are as we are,
time-trapped, and because our images of ourselves
and the facts of ourselves wake at night and bicker
and lay bets with one another, with us as the stakes.

Then moved to pity at last because we hear and are saddened—
Nearly beautiful in the occasions of our pity not of
ourselves. Nearly affectionate when we are free of pain.

Caught as we are in these and our other conditions—
Which include a distaste for the littleness of our motives,
and, therefore, some wish to live toward some reality.
Terrified by realities. Addicted to evasions. Daring, perhaps
once, to look into the mirror and see and not look away.

Beginning again, then, with those who share with us and with whom
we share the sorrows of the common failure.
Fumbling at last to the language of a sympathy
that can describe, and that will be, we are persuaded,
sufficiently joy when we find in one another its idioms.

Caught as we are in these defining conditions—
I wish you the one fact of ourselves that is inexhaustible
and which, therefore, we need not horde nor begrudge.
Let mercy be its name till its name be found.
And wish that to the mercy that is possible because it takes
nothing from us and may, therefore, be given indifferently,
there be joined the mercy that adds us to one another.

Put stone steps anywhere and time sets in.
Builders make steps climb. Time takes them down.
Look at Rome's warped stones. Every man,
woman, child, going up to pray scuffs the stone
one soul thinner. Before it's gone
workmen come by and lay a new one.
But only a stop-gap. Begin again
anywhere: you only begin again. The first foot on
the block is the last begun.
What's done is not done instantly, but it *is* done.

There gets to be less and less to climb by—to prayer
or to anything. If workmen do not get there
in time you find a ramp instead of a stair.
If no one gets there, you find a mound where
the ramp was and nothing on top. Why *are*
stones thought to be solids? Air
is as long. It is only faster than they. Rarer
but not less firm. Air, moreover, can repair
itself. What stone can? And you can climb higher
on air than on stone. If you're
out for altitude, build accordingly. If you dare.

WHOLLY NUMBERS
or
THE MEDITATIONS OF ST. STITCH

Meditations of Saint Stitch

I.

I do not make my life. I am neither
guilty nor innocent of it. It occurs to me,
and I find myself in the occurrence. Another
animal might die of what frees me or go free
in what I die of. There is this
world whose lives go thus-and-thus,

its animals, each shaped to the food of its kind,
its men and women, each shaped to some imagining
of what has been done to each. A few half-blind
gods, or their statuaries, stand aging in
the weathers of the look one takes at this world,
but surely the rank red foxes of the last wood

will den in every altar. Is heaven their haven
then? It is of stones to be left behind
and of foxes to sleep in stone places. Because I am given
to musings, I muse. Somehow I found
a habit of small successes. They flow.
They do not flower. What is the flaw

in us that lets in the trivial? It is so much
easier to be impressive than to be,
to sound than to say, to march
steeled to nothing than to saunter by
windings nowhere to, perhaps, at last,
something a self finds being cheerfully lost.

II.

Because I am given to working, I work.
Because words find me, I go to find
words, the food of my kind. I walk

by nowheres to the luck of a word, its found
wild honey. A good night is a forest
in which bee-trees are, the sweetness and the blackrust

of dead wood bled together. Is there a meaning
to the taste of things? to that sweet-soiled
best of honey, tangy with woodrot's moss-morning
whiff of old wet? Words are as sullied
a sweet as any bear claws from dead wood.
(Ignoring, because he is furred for it, the cloud

of sharp nuisances that boils to distract him.
He has his feast-at-a-time. Then the next thing
happens, and the next. He sways home
to his winter rocks. You could hear him sing
there, if you dared his waking. Bears are great
snorers. They are the beast of that.)

Have words a meaning? This so-to-speak forest
in which I do nothing till my luck works
is leafed with sayings. I listen. The first
man's food is a word. Speaking, he wakes,
no longer animal and said-to, but himself
the sayer of what he hears, not safe

now anywhere. He has ripped the dead wood
and with the flawed sweet on his tongue learns
he is not furred for the boiling cloud
he has let out. Let *him* think what it means.
I think the words he thinks with—
that they are wider upon him than all wrath.

"Nothing Is Really Hard but to Be Real—"

—Now let me tell you why I said that.
Try to put yourself into an experimental mood.
Stop right here and try to review everything
you felt about that line. Did you accept it
as wisdom? as perception? as a gem, maybe,
for your private anthology of Telling Truths?

My point is that the line is fraudulent.
A blurb. It is also relevant that I know
at least a dozen devoutly intellectual
journals that will gladly buy any fourteen
such lines plus a tinny rhyme scheme and
compound the felony by calling that a sonnet.

—Very well, then, I am a cynic. Though, for
the record, let me add that I am a cynic with
one wife, three children, and other invest-
ments. Whoever heard of a cynic carrying a
pack for the fun of it? It won't really do.
I'm something else.
                    Were I to dramatize myself,
I'd say I am a theologian who keeps meeting
the devil as a master of make-up, and that
among his favorite impersonations he appears,
often as not, as the avuncular old ham who winks,
tugs his ear, and utters such gnomic garbage
as: "Nothing is really hard but to be real."

I guess what the devil gets out of this—if he is
the fool he seems to be—is the illusion of
imitating heaven. If, on the other hand, he is no
fool, then his deceptions are carefully practiced

and we are all damned. For all of us, unless
we are carefully warned, will accept such noises
as examples of the sound an actual mind makes.

Why are we damned then? —I am glad you asked that.
It is, as we say to flatter oafs, a good question.
(Meaning, usually, the one we were fishing for. Good.)
In any case, I may now pretend to think out the answer
I have memorized:
                    We are damned for accepting as
the sound a man makes, the sound of something else,
thereby losing the truth of our own sound.
                                        How do we
learn our own sound? (Another good question. Thank you.)
—by listening to what men there have been and are
—by reading more poets than jurists (without scorning
Law) —and by reading what we read not for its
oration, but for its resemblance to that sound in which
we best hear most of what a man is. Get that sound into
your heads and you will know what tones to exclude.

—*if* there is enough exclusion in you to keep the
pie plates out of the cymbals, the tin horns out of
the brass section, the baling wire out of the strings,
and thereby to let the notes roll full to the ear
that has listened enough to be a listener.

As for the devil—when he has finished every imp-
ersonation, the best he will have been able to accomplish
is only that sound which is exactly *not* the music.

A diagrammed angel, robed in principles,
sequences, and conclusions, modeled for me
the possible creations.
                              Articles of faith
veiled him at first. A tapestry
of declarations shimmered shut behind him.
And the first creation was a lit hand pointing—
as Michelangelo had designed it. The angel
walked through absences, and behind him,
at every step, birds and foliages painted
a world in place. The naked swell
of man to woman yearned on the motion of his
caftan. He carried a pack and wore new sandals.

The second creation was all white on white.
The curtains behind him, and he before them,
were exactly those absences he had first walked
trailing a world into place that he might walk it.

I signaled him to go on. The third creation
burst against a backdrop of white peaks,
sun-topped, and browsed by humped goats. A lace
of jeweled allusions cascaded. Cloud packs
of ideas spiraled about him in a lit chase
between the changeling shelves of heaven and earth,
doing for men what men could not do for themselves.

There were many more. All pictorial and enjoyable.
One, an adaptation of harem dress. One,
dust colored as the floor of a stable.
One, like armor, but made of linked bone,
Germanic and rank in feeling. There is no room

to mention them all, nor his staging of them.
I was, in fact, about to conclude that it was all,
at best, interesting, when the curtain divided
a last time and he stood naked. Not visible—not
exactly—but in place there in the colliding
voids of his diagram, particled, inconceivably ordinary,
himself his own background over and over and over.

The Day I Bought the Biggest Car in the World

The day I bought the biggest car in the world
I had nowhere to go. The afternoon rained itself
blind. Norman Cousins didn't get back from
Washington. His girl Dori called to cancel
our golf date. But the rain had already done that.
Then the cloud burst did burst itself out, eased,
and I took Judith to New York and dinner. We got
last minute seats to "Who's Afraid of Edward Albee?"
and watched the actors invent lives out of
what had been written with no lives in it.
Nancy Kelly, playing Martha, looked like one
woman we knew, acted a little like another, and more
like another. Arthur Hill looked like himself
and made that look almost like a life. Good actors.
Nothing was missing from them but an author.

By almost midnight it had almost cleared and then did.
But the instant we had the car out of the garage
it started again. Judith patted our spang red
leather interior and said, "Well, it's watertight."
I practically put my nose through the windshield
trying to see where we were going. But not even our
analogue, synchro-swipe, shur-power, everlast wipers
could get the rain out of the way. I followed
streaks of red light under the river—where, for a while,
the dark was visible again—then up again to the red-
streaked blindness. One dome of red had a truck in it,
over on its side. Two police cars transmitted red-code
from their beacons. A wrecker, like a praying mantis,
nibbled at the wreck but could not eat it. Then dark again,
streaked red. I closed my eyes and prayed to Treasury
to show my tax structure its way. When I opened them again

it was morning. I was in my own bed, my wife beside me
like the fruit and bread of goodmorning on white cloths.
"Wherever *is* there to go," I thought. I lay in the first bed
of this life again with nothing to go to but what came to me.

At the window, morning was having one of God's birthdays
in the thicket. Jays and cardinals had come to be its candles.
In God's honor, for the birthday of all thickets, we lay
archaic and glad in the hour all Bibles begin with.

After breakfast I found the white glare of our chariot
spattered with red tears. I, or whatever had brought us home,
had forgotten, and parked it under the wild cherry in its
dripping August. And still it glared white-and-chrome,
though blood-streaked, offending the thicket and its candles.
And I kicked one whitewall to scuff it, and gardened all
    morning.

Possibilities

A week ago on longer clocks than ours
a supernova in Orion lit
the sky like a full moon. The dinosaurs
might have looked up and made a note of it
but didn't, and the next night it blinked out.
The next day from a metaphoric tree
my father's father's beetle brow and snout
poked through the leaves. Just yesterday at three
he spoke his first word. And an hour ago
invented God. And, in the last hour, Doubt.

I, because my only clock's too slow
for less than hope, hope he will not fall out
of time and space at least for one more week
of the long clock. Think, given time enough,
what languages he might yet learn to speak
when the last hairs have withered from his scruff,
when his dark brows unknit and he looks out,
when the last ape has grunted from his throat.

Styles

Assuming, in some dreamscape, some
stylist past the domeless dome
whose metaphors, asprawl, include
the dark in which first gases brood
and hatch the star-shower billion years
between what blinks and disappears—

and then, assuming that this dust
on one fleck of the outer crust
of one arm of one galaxy
gets up and walks—like you, like me—
and in, perhaps, the million years
before it blinks and disappears

develops some style of its own
beginning with light, water, stone.
And, now, say that first stylist chose
to write a universe—there it is.
Can we, as stylists, read that style
but from ourselves, and for a while,

before there is no style like ours
to read at all, and the star showers
fall on unread, their text asprawl
on everything and after all,
when no one's left to try to spell
what none of us read very well

to start with?
                    Well, enough of this.
A universe is a lot to miss.
But our not missing it won't be missed.
While there is time, it's time we kissed.
What time's left over drifts asprawl
on really nothing after all.

It was snowing. The bodies of women
walked through the bone rooms
of insomnia. A white madman's attic in the skull
became their promenade deck. In a mirror
facing the prefrontal lobe, like a door
to a time machine, a ballroom of old Saint
Petersburg glittered with snow and nudity.

It was snowing on the bodies of women
in the tesseract at the edge of the space-warp
in the bone-mind of the madman's insomnia.
From the bridge of a Grace Liner under the Southern Cross
the Captain led an orchestra in the bows.
Women swayed their frosted thighs in a conga.
A red bull from the sea clawed at the rail,

burst through the snow and music,
and took command of the ship, smashing the mirror
from the Captain's skull. The ship instantly
spun down the vortex behind the music, and the snow
fell on the bodies of women who would not be indifferent
but slid from bed to bed through all the sea,
leaving a corpse in every bed they rumpled.

Blue

In its window high in the hotel fronting the Gulf
the sky kept sorting its lights and letting them fall.
Light after light across those waters, blue
performed all its possibilities from morning
into the blaze before night. A cross section
of sea-time: blue and the histories of blue.
At day's end I could recall blue systems banded
like rock strata, telling the age of each light
and what lives moved in the blue plains then.

Gulls stained blue by the ages they sailed on
cruised from bed to bed of that light. Seas
swelled into its changes and broke frothy. A sail
rose dingy at the shore and drew away
into a dazzle so sharp it cut through to
the mother of blue in every whiteness.
There was nothing in all those ages-made-visible
but blue was stained into the grain and core of it.
To remember time at all was to see again

the presence of blue principle, and the lives
flickering there, and adrift at the blue edges.
And gone like weather. Oh it was not for nothing
that great fop, Sandro Botticelli, combed
and curled the sea and called a lady simpering
out of the foam as if from a hairdresser
so suave he made an art of tousling. She comes
like the blaze before nightfall to the blue-struck bone
of the man stripped of himself. She is his weather come.

Long as the light changes in its huge window,
she flames from blue, and the sea lies down in curls.

Museum

Dig up the stones any lost empire has worked on
and set them in the vaults and the long halls—
you see the faces of a monumental imagination.
Every ruin says of them that they had the idea
of being man confused with the idea of being God.

Open their tombs for trinkets and propitiations—
you see that they loved life so hard they meant
always to take it with them. These bones are
the children of bone. Boxed in faith, the thought
they were lies wound to the fine dust of their legend.

Walk out of any museum to the unsaved stones
of the city that is there, its brummagem traffic
of ambitions. Have these lives changed their waiting?
Is there a face to this imagination? Is that a soul
hailing a taxi? Will the chariot come afire?

They believe yet, the relics of this outer vault.
The stones will be scratched again and again
with the names their ruin cries, waiting forever
in the necropolis of which time is no suburb
and from which there is no service to the city;

there in the Stone Age of the dark to say over and over and
over that it is not comfort enough to be a man,
that only what is endless is purposeful or even
bearable, that time is no city to keep to but only
the entrance into the City of all Monuments.

The Starry Heavens, the Moral Law

Kant saw them as the two eternal sources of awe:
the starry heavens above, the moral law within.
Both of which it is possible to doubt, but, all in all,
impossible not to have thought about. Stated as Law:
everyone would like Heaven as a second skin.

We know we are here and small at the outskirts of
some fabulous system we sense above and far off,
we of this grainy planet of this pebbly sun
at the pelagic fringe, who dreamed ourselves once
the size and center, and called it Father and Love.

And we sense we are related to one another
by some compact whose terms we all forever
puzzle at, wander from, but return to, and must again,
from every loss of phrasing and abdication
of ourselves. And think to call that, Man.

Take it for awe if you like. Whatever we mean *is*
in a dimension like truth, as we dream it. But awe
is the invention of ourselves. Call the compact Law;
call those lights Heaven; but add this:
they are themselves nothing. They imagine *us.*

No, not even that. It is we who imagine them
imagining us. Another species might have been born
blind and found its awe in the unseen edges of stone,
or in the endless peeling and reunion of a stream
around a dipped hand. Anything can find its dream

in anything: it is there to be found. What made
stars more than rock and water? Whatever we are born to,
a mystery will follow. We do

need one another. The rest we adapt to. Mud
is heaven enough for crocodiles. Suppose we grew

senses for the motion of roots under us? heard waves
of one another's thoughts? or the breaking of flesh in graves?
We should build ourselves then to such hearkenings,
live in them, find our mysteries and imaginings
in them. And still we should need those things

and one another. Separation is the one death. As life is
the fitting and refitting of what we shall never quite
join. We are—and what are we? Found wrong. Lost right.
Floundering and in love. All of us, somewhere. Meaningless?
No. Only—unsayable to ourselves. Though I might

say most of it for myself if you would carve it
over my head at the speaking time: *Thank you*
for the experience which I, lovingly, did not
understand. And not to waste good stone, a usable plot,
nor any love, let me beg that if you do

honor my wish, you make my stone a bench. Anyone
who will stop by another man's life may need to sit down.

A Genesis

All day the boom wind swung against the shore
   battering the swells to fog, then fell away.
   The sea lay down and panted like a dog
   after a chase. The gulls came out like flies.
   Boys flexed their polyp toes into the sand
   by river systems one day old
   through continents already one day gone.

It was again the first-held easy summer
   after the hurl of heaven made the world
   and the sea lay down in place in its idea,
   and the children of dominion walked the shore
   each in his kind. And on the western rim
   angels leaned dreaming on their burning swords,
   before they turned and began to be forgotten.

Oh were there ghosts even in that first summer
   before the dog lay down and dragged his breath?
   Slipshod, easy, affluent in its rhymes
   the sea was there, shouldering imagination
   and shrugging it to time. I saw the boys
   pause and grow thin as mist on their white bones,
   the sea made visible in their first look.

Principles

In the zoo of God's imagination,
by the first principle of the cruising shark's
all-baling mouth, I firm

a thought that sees. By shapes that turn to stone
avast in the runnels and darks
of beds of exhaled seas. By the worm

screwed blind into the worm and whale.
By the factory of the mammoth stopped.
By the nit clinging to Cause

in the wattles of the lizard, and the trail
laid egg to egg to the flip-flopped
end and beginning in the rumpled Laws,

I stay told, reasonless, we must find
moment in one another, or never.
—By the incredible made diet. By the unbearable

made custom. By the worm made mind
to think its eggs to nothing and forever.
By the maunder of all energy to its fall.

The Colossus in Quicksand

One night I read philosophy.
When Plato went to sleep on me
I made this dream up willfully:

I saw a stone colossus rise
from Lybian sands through the Nine Skies.
Someone's idea of something's size—

man's of a man, I seemed to know.
I couldn't force the dream to go
so close that a whole truth might show.

Still it went near enough to guess
it wasn't some high mightiness.
No emperor or emperess

ever had slaves enough or stones
breaking each other from the bones
of time enough, though it were aeons,

to haul so much of earth so high.
The figure stretched from sand to sky.
Its very height, at first, was why

no one had noticed it was sinking.
Only a dream could see it shrinking—
or so I dreamed the dream was thinking.

One sky after another cleared
to nothing as the great head neared.
Shins, then kneecaps disappeared.

It slid like weather from the skies.
Thighs, the great sex in the thighs,
the first rib—then I saw its eyes.

Whatever the thing was meant to be,
all Greece and Rome intended me
to look into its eyes and see.

I watched the chest and then the chin
go under, and the sands begin
to rim the mouth and trickle in.

Then it was eye to eye, and then
the desert was all sand again,
a nothing where a dream had been.

And what I saw as it went by
was its own image in its eye
still standing higher than the sky.

Men at Their Pace of Hours

Men at their pace of hours
pause into time. A suddenness
looks at the world and its habits of glory
slide down a rayed sky, or, from no sky,
snow-wicks light all day and again
all day and again till
cities surrender as the line breaks
between coming and going. Then,
out of errands, the man is
the newness of himself employed,
his unknown act of being
arrested among moonscapes—
the crescent rims and bone-salt craters,
the ram's horns at the eaves of thought,
the void's robed angels raying
their trumps through nothing, seen.

From the hour of the impossible act comes the bare-handed
  hero
in skins of strangled polar bears, not even frostbitten.
From the hour of the most possible thought, looks back the
  wracked man,
his eyes hunting calms there are words for, a while.
Between doing and having done all men have their hours told.

Great contests engage the memory. Björnsen, in fact, did
leap on an ice cake and kill a polar bear with a dagger
and desperation, living to eat it and wear it. And Job
crouched cradling forever in his braised arms the little bodies
slashed from his love, and waited and waited for God's point.

It was Björnsen who went on. Watching from hiding,
the Eskimos who had stolen his boat witnessed the act
by what they knew of God-touched possibility, and next
  morning
the boat was back in place. Could God in *His* hiding
unbutcher Job's children and make a next thing happen?

From an hour in time comes the not-very-good train
that takes us, a bit grimy, to even perhaps the extraordinary.
From the hour after time the man waits forever by
a rusted track in weeds, thinking the source of his thoughts.
All hours can be entered. Not all can be ended.